# EDUCATION IN JAPAN: INSIGHTS AND REFLECTIONS FROM MY VISIT

## DR DHEERAJ MEHROTRA

# Contents

# Preface

Education in Japan has long been praised for its ability to combine academic success with strong moral values and life skills. As an educator and lifelong learner, I've always been intrigued by how different countries tackle the task of preparing young brains for an increasingly complex world. This desire prompted me to learn more about Japan's educational system during my recent visit as part of a team from Kunwar's Global School in Lucknow. The experience was nothing short of transforming, giving me a deep knowledge of how education can develop a student's intellect, character, values, and sense of duty.

The journey into Japan's classrooms, teacher training centres, and learning spaces allowed me to see firsthand how their educational concept is implemented. Japan's unique approach to education, which combines modern technical developments with age-old traditions of discipline and respect, struck me as a model worthy of further study and imitation. This book attempts to impart the insights I gathered during my tour, focussing on the techniques and concepts that make Japan's education system so effective and comprehensive.

One of the main themes I noticed throughout my tour was a focus on balance. In Japanese education, academic accomplishment and moral growth are equally important. Students are instructed to excel in areas such as mathematics, physics, and languages and encouraged to be respectful, responsible, and community-oriented. In a world where the need to excel academically can frequently eclipse the importance of personal development, Japan provides a welcome reminder of the importance of teaching the complete person.

Another important factor that affected the situation was the respect shown to instructors in Japan. The **sensei** (teacher) job is highly valued, and continuing professional development is an essential component of the education system. This commitment to raising teaching standards through collaboration and reflective methods such as **lesson study** creates a robust framework from which other countries, including India, can benefit.

In this book, I look at several fundamental aspects of the Japanese education system, including its planned and balanced curriculum, emphasis on moral education, technological integration, and teacher professionalism. As India implements its National Education Policy (NEP) 2020, we can learn many lessons from Japan's approach. Whether it's instilling a sense of duty and respect in kids or establishing a supportive environment for instructors, Japan provides a model that resonates with the goals of educators worldwide.

This book is more than just a description of my trip to Japan; it is a call to action for educators, policymakers, and parents. As we work to establish educational systems that educate kids about tomorrow's problems, we must learn from successful models such as Japan's. The insights provided here are intended to spark contemplation and discussion about how we may build education to be more than just a means of achievement but also a foundation for ethical, responsible, and well-rounded persons.

I hope this book is helpful for educators and readers committed to improving education and creating systems that nurture each student's mind, body, and soul.

-- Dr Dheeraj Mehrotra
   www.authordheerajmehrotra.com

A visit to Tokyo as an educationist is undoubtedly a remarkable and enlightening experience. Tokyo, being a hub of innovation and cultural richness, offers invaluable insights into a balanced, forward-thinking education system that seamlessly integrates tradition with modern advancements. As an educationist, observing the Japanese education system firsthand provides lessons not just in academic excellence but also in the holistic development of students.

# ONE

# THE STRUCTURE OF THE JAPANESE EDUCATION SYSTEM

"Better than a thousand days of diligent study is one day with a great teacher" is a Japanese proverb that highlights the importance of a great teacher.

## Introduction

*Education in Japan is widely regarded as one of the world's most efficient and successful systems, marked by a unique blend of traditional values, innovative methodologies, and a deep respect for learning. My visit to Japan as part of a delegation from Kunwar's Global School, Lucknow, gave me first-hand insights into the educational practices that shape the minds of future generations in Japan. This book aims to document and share my observations and reflections on the Japanese education system. It focuses on its key features, strengths, and areas that offer learning opportunities for other educational models, including India.*

## The Structure of the Japanese Education System

*The Japanese education system is highly organized and structured. It is divided into several key stages:*

*1. Elementary School (Shōgakkō) – Six years*
*2. Lower Secondary School (Chūgakkō) – Three years*
*3. Upper Secondary School (Kōtōgakkō) – Three*

*years*

*4.    University    (Daigaku)    or    Vocational Education (Senmon Gakkō) – Two to four years*

*The compulsory education period lasts nine years and covers elementary and lower secondary education. Throughout this period, emphasis is placed on academic proficiency, moral education, and the development of social skills.*

*I observed a seamless integration of traditional values with modern teaching methodologies during my visit to elementary and secondary schools in Tokyo and Kyoto. Respect for elders, discipline, and a sense of responsibility are deeply embedded in the school culture. At the same time, schools are embracing technology and innovation to equip students with 21ˢᵗ-century skills.*

*Japan's education system is internationally renowned for its discipline, academic rigour, and holistic approach to developing well-rounded individuals. During my visit to Japan as part of a delegation from Kunwar's Global School, Lucknow, I had the unique opportunity to experience their educational framework's intricacies. This journey offered valuable insights into the practices, philosophies, and systems that make Japanese education stand out. Reflecting on this visit, I found numerous elements of the Japanese education system that could serve as valuable lessons for educational reform in India.*

Ask a question and you feel shame for a moment. Not asking and not knowing means you will feel shame for your whole life" is a Japanese quote that encourages people to ask questions and not be afraid to admit they don't know something.

## Structured and Balanced Approach

*The Japanese education system follows a well-organized structure, focusing on building strong foundational knowledge during the compulsory nine years of schooling (six years of elementary and three years of lower secondary). What sets this structure apart is its balance between academic achievement and character development. Each school day is meticulously planned, ensuring students engage in various activities, from academics to extracurriculars.*

*What stood out was the integration of practical life skills and moral education into the curriculum. For example, students in Japan actively participate in cleaning their classrooms and school premises, fostering a sense of responsibility and respect for their environment. This practice, known as **O-soji**, is something that Indian schools could quickly adopt to instil discipline and communal responsibility from a young age.*

A Japanese proverb that emphasizes that learning is a gradual process and that patience and time are needed to fully understand new information.

# TWO

# A Day in the Life of a Japanese Student

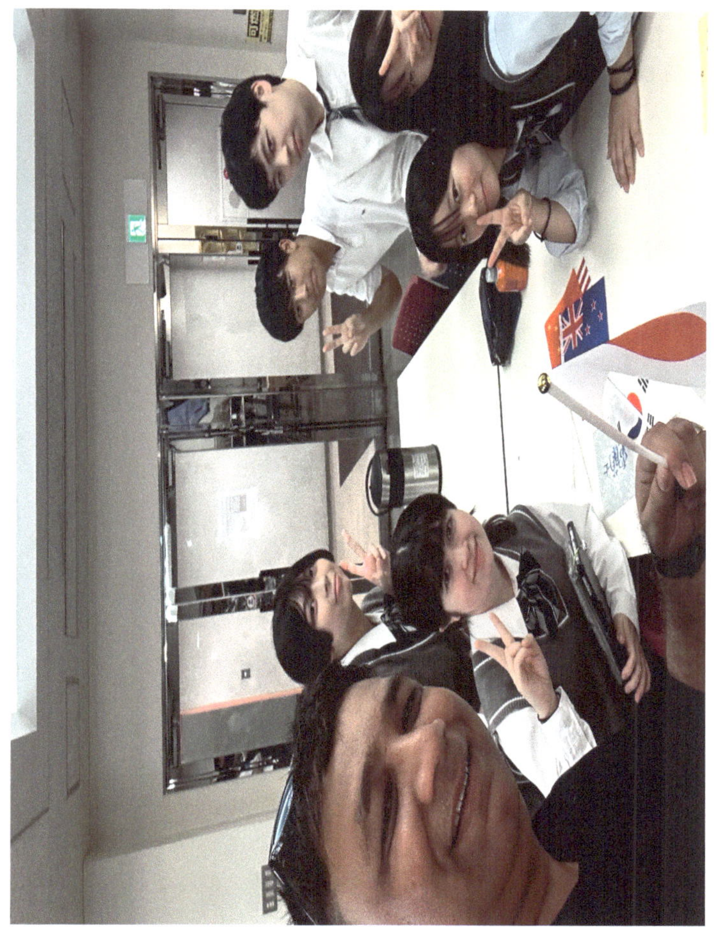

If you talk to a man in a language he understands, that goes to his head. If you talk to him in his own language, that goes to his heart.

*Among the most notable characteristics of the Japanese educational system is that students are expected to live in a disciplined and regulated manner. Students are immersed in an environment designed to teach them values such as punctuality, responsibility, and teamwork from the minute they begin their school day until the time they leave in the afternoon. I observed how these characteristics are taught through various school activities, many firmly entrenched in Japanese culture. This was something that I witnessed throughout my trip to Japan. A fundamental topic that contributes to the general development of pupils is the emphasis placed on self-discipline and group harmony. This subject plays a significant role in shaping the daily experiences of students.*

## The Organising of the School Morning

*Students in Japan often begin their day at an early hour, and they frequently participate in a morning assembly. Significant announcements are delivered during this assembly, and students are typically encouraged to reflect on their objectives for the day. The day will be filled with academic classes, club activities, and community duties; this planned beginning will set the tone for the day. The Japanese style of education, in contrast to many other educational systems, which emphasise academics, incorporates life skills into the daily routine. This ensures that students acquire knowledge and develop crucial personal and social skills.*

*Both how students approach their studies and extracurricular activities demonstrate the importance of timeliness and responsibility. Students are expected to be on time for academics and extracurricular events, and tardiness is strongly discouraged. As students learn to manage their time efficiently, balance their duties, and strive towards their goals with attention and determination, they develop a feeling of discipline that they carry over into their personal lives.*

The great remedy for ignorance ... is knowledge of languages

*The practice of cleaning is referred to as O-shoji.*

*O-soji, also known as cleaning time, is a tradition considered one of the most distinctive and admirable in Japanese schools. The students are responsible for cleaning their classrooms, hallways, and any other school sections available during this period. This exercise is not only a job; it is an essential component of the school day aimed at educating kids about the significance of contributing to the community and the importance of being accountable for their actions and respecting their surroundings.*

*O-shoji instils a sense of ownership in pupils since they are directly accountable for maintaining the cleanliness and orderliness of their environment. This gives them a sense of responsibility. This practice encourages the concept that the school is a shared area and that everyone is responsible for contributing to the maintenance of the school. Students appreciate cleanliness, discipline, and teamwork by participating in this daily practice. In addition, it reaffirms that success in life is not solely dependent on academic accomplishments but also on accepting responsibility for one's actions and the environment in which one resides.*

Knowledge of languages is the doorway to wisdom.

*The term **"Bukatsu"** refers to extracurricular activities and clubs.*

*Japanese schools place significant importance on extracurricular activities,* **bukatsu,** *and an organized academic schedule. Whether in athletics, the arts, music, or other cultural endeavours, students are strongly encouraged to join organisations catering to their specific interests. Outside of the classroom, students can improve skills through participation in these clubs, which meet regularly and frequently occur beyond school hours.*

"everyone [in a group] is not only supposed to think and act alike, they are also supposed to be equal in ability" from "Kata" by Lafayette De Mente (2003)

*Club membership helps students feel more connected to one another and develops a sense of belonging in the community. Students who participate in these activities understand the significance of endurance, leadership, and cooperation. The greater emphasis on group harmony observed across Japanese society is mirrored by the sense of community that develops within these clubs. Students form deep friendships with their classmates due to the activities in which they collaborate to accomplish shared objectives.*

*The Japanese educational system takes a comprehensive approach to ensure that students in Japan are not simply focused on academic performance. Academic performance is essential; nevertheless, it should be balanced with possibilities for personal development gained through extracurricular activities. Because of this balance, the children are more prepared for the obstacles they will face after school, which helps them build well-rounded personalities.*

"Contrary to myth, Japan is not a single, monolithic culture persistently characterized by harmony and consensus...Rather, Japan is a nation of complex subcultures and has a plurality of traditions that have undergone considerable change over time... nowhere is this past better seen than in the repeated controversies about schooling over the past 150 years." Learning to be Modern, Byron K Marshall

## *Lessons for Other Educational Systems In the World*

*The structure and discipline seen in Japanese schools can provide helpful lessons for various educational systems, especially the ones practised in India. Schools can assist children in developing the life skills that are important for success by emphasizing values such as punctuality, responsibility, and teamwork. Students can be encouraged to feel responsible and ownership over their learning environment by including techniques such as O-soji in the school day. This practice can also encourage students to take pleasure in their learning environment.*

*In addition, the importance of holistic development is brought to light because extracurricular activities are seen as vital components of the educational process. Students should be allowed to explore their interests, develop their talents, and form close relationships with their classmates as part of their education. Education should not be limited to academics alone.*

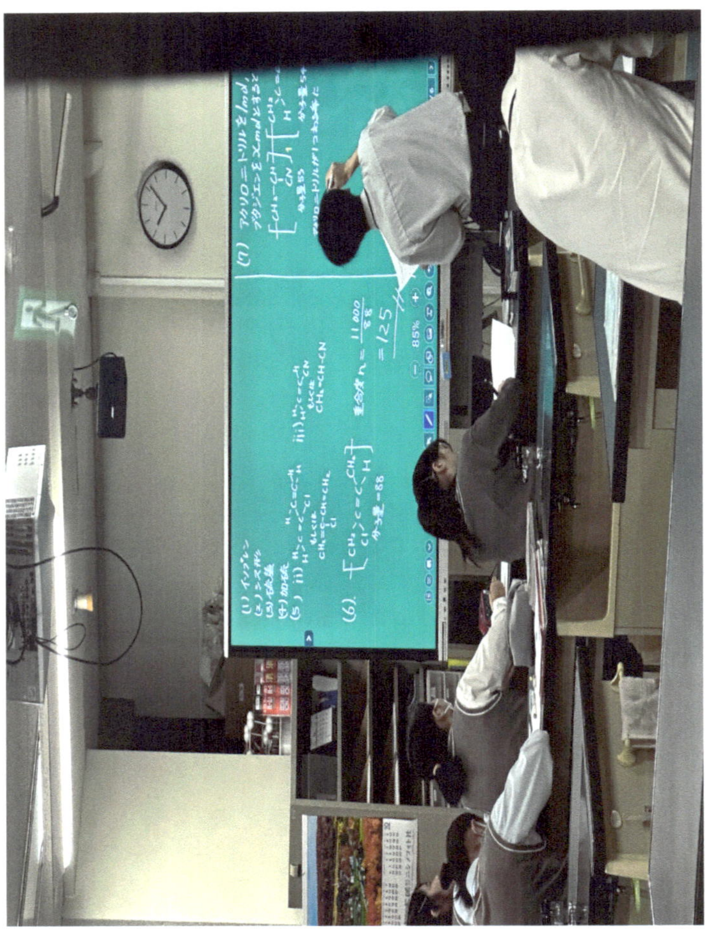

"In the 1990's, respected university researchers claimed that the Japanese were genetically unique in their ability to appreciate to the fullest the sounds of nature like crickets and waterfalls" Insight Guides Japan

*The educational system in Japan serves as a paradigm for how the concepts of responsibility, discipline, and teamwork can be effectively incorporated into the context of the academic experience. Japanese kids develop academically and personally through regimented daily routines, practices such as O-shoji, and a significant emphasis on extracurricular activities to supplement their education. The execution of these activities results in the development of well-rounded persons who are ready to make a constructive contribution to society. These insightful insights from Japan offer valuable direction on building a more balanced and holistic approach to education, particularly relevant when other countries, including India, are working to change their educational systems.*

*The Japanese educational system strongly focuses on personal responsibility and community ideals, which are represented in various aspects of student life. These*

*components include laws regarding personal possessions and clothing codes. Even though the precise practices regarding personal goods and apparel may vary significantly from one school to the next, the fundamental principles of safety, respect for shared places, and practicality are consistent across the Japanese education system. By comparing these values to the Japanese system, one can better understand how schools worldwide handle specific areas of student life. These values align with the information offered at KIS (Kyoto International School) regarding personal things and dress requirements.*

*Personal Items: Taking Responsibility and Practicing Minimalism*

*Students in Japan are often discouraged from bringing unneeded personal items to school, similar to the guidelines discussed for KIS. Schooling in Japan strongly emphasises teaching pupils how to deal with what is required of them, particularly in the early years of their education. This helps kids develop a feeling of responsibility and discipline. Toys, electronic devices, and other personal possessions are frequently disallowed because they have the potential to take away from the learning experience. In addition, schools expect that students would respect community spaces and refrain from engaging in activities such as trade or bartering, which could result in misunderstandings or confrontations between classmates.*

*There is a strong resonance between the Japanese emphasis on personal accountability and the policy at KIS that emphasises the school's lack of responsibility for the loss or theft of individual items. As a reflection of the more considerable cultural value that is placed on respect for shared surroundings, students in Japan are instructed to take care of their possessions and to adhere to the rules that are in place within the classroom. To foster an atmosphere that is more conducive to learning than acquiring material belongings, Japanese schools and KIS have taken measures to limit the usage of personal items and toys.*

*The Dress Code:*

*Striking a Balance Between Individual Expression and Official Clothing*

*While KIS is currently a non-uniform school, there have been conversations about the possibility of implementing uniforms. However, Japanese schools are internationally recognised for their strict adherence to the requirement that students wear school uniforms. When it comes to school culture, uniforms are considered to be an essential component in Japan. They serve to promote equality and reduce distractions that are based on personal appearance. In addition, they are considered a means of instilling a sense of discipline and belonging in students under Japan's greater emphasis on community and communal harmony.*

*Japanese schools allow for a certain amount of flexibility and practicality regarding their clothing requirements. For instance, students frequently switch into various clothes for specialised activities such as physical education or cleaning their classrooms. Similar to the KIS policy that requires students to have distinct apparel for physical education and field trips, these specialised uniforms ensure that pupils are always dressed appropriately for the activity. Both systems are designed to prioritise practicality and safety to guarantee that children can learn and move around throughout their school day.*

*As a practice mirrored in the KIS requirement for two pairs of shoes, the use of shoes appropriate for indoor and outdoor use is one of the distinguishing characteristics of Japanese schools. When children enter a school building in Japan, they are expected to change into indoor slippers or shoes. This is a requirement. Because dirt and trash from the outside are kept out of classrooms and gymnasiums, this approach helps to maintain a clean environment. Additionally, it teaches students how to keep the classroom atmosphere clean and respectful at all times. Similarly, the KIS policy, which mandates that students bring two pairs of shoes to school, ensures that classrooms are kept clean and that students are adequately equipped for activities that require physical activity. This practice also helps reinforce safety by ensuring that children are always wearing footwear that is appropriate for the situation in an emergency.*

## Clothing that is both Comfortable and Safe to Wear

*Regarding the clothing students are permitted to wear, Japanese dress regulations are often highly stringent, emphasising modesty and safety. The strategy taken by KIS, which gives students the freedom to select their attire within a broad range of constraints, provides more flexibility than the conventional Japanese educational system. Despite this, both systems have the same fundamental objectives: clothing should be functional, secure, and favourable to learning experiences. In Japan, there should be no showy accessories or apparel that could potentially distract from the studying process. Similarly, the Kingdom of Japan School bans attire that contains unsuitable language or images.*

*Both systems emphasize safety measures regarding footwear. The KIS's restriction on flip-flops and high heels for emergency reasons reflects the safety-conscious ethos of Japanese schools. In Japanese schools, pupils are expected to wear shoes that allow them to move quickly and safely during an evacuation or other emergency.*

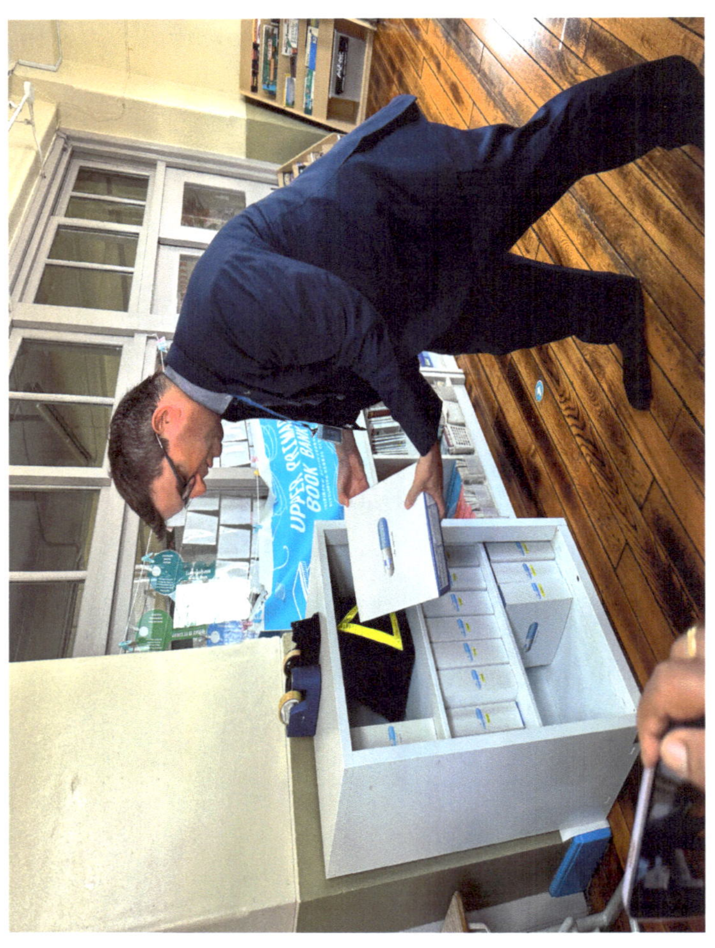

*Although there are some differences between the*

*Japanese education system and the KIS regarding the specifics of personal things and clothing rules, the two approaches share the core ideals of responsibility, safety, and pragmatism. The Japanese system strongly emphasises discipline, conformity, and respect for shared spaces, which is evident in its restrictions on personal possessions and clothes.*

*On the other hand, the KIS balances these ideals by taking a more laid-back attitude to individual expression. The objective of both systems, on the other hand, is to establish a well-organised, secure, and focused learning environment that allows students to grow intellectually and personally.*

# THREE

## THE ROLE OF TEACHERS

"Education in Japan is not intended to create people accomplished in the techniques of the arts and sciences, but rather to manufacture the persons required by the State" Arinori Mori, Japan's first education minister, quoted by Patrick Smith

*Japanese teachers, known as "sensei," play a significant role in their pupils' intellectual and moral development through their teaching.*

*In Japan, the relationship between teachers and students is characterised by mutual respect, and teachers are seen as role models for the students responsible for educating. Teachers in Japan regularly invest additional time in activities such as lesson planning, grading assignments, and engaging in self-reflection as part of their commitment to continual professional development. This is done to foster a culture of continuous improvement.*

*The extremely high level of respect and professionalism shown to teachers in the Japanese educational system is one of the most distinguishing characteristics of this system. There is a significant difference between the position of a teacher in Japan, known as a "sensei," and that of an academic instructor. Students look up to their teachers as mentors, guides, and role models because they make a substantial contribution to the overall development of their students. This deeply ingrained cultural regard for educators is accompanied by a solid system of continual professional development, guaranteeing that the highest possible teaching quality standards are maintained.*

"Rote learning is the child's next lesson in dependence. To think is an act of autonomy: to memorize the given is to rely on authority" Patrick Smith

## The Function Played by Educators in Japan.

*Teachers in Japan are tasked not only with the responsibility of teaching knowledge to their students but also with the responsibility of influencing their pupils' moral and social values. This is a positive development under Japan's emphasis on character development as an essential education component. Japanese society places a high value on virtues such as responsibility, empathy, and discipline, and teachers must instil these values in their students. Consequently, teachers in Japan are entrusted with a substantial amount of responsibility, as shown by the high level of respect they receive from students, parents, and the community.*

"Order, discipline, self-control; it is the school rather than the family which is largely responsible for building these elements into the masculine Japanese character."
Ronald P Dore

*Further institutionalisation of this respect may be seen in how teachers are supported throughout their careers. In the Japanese educational system, significant emphasis is placed on the importance of professionalism and continuous learning for teachers. Through implementing a systematic approach to continued professional development, educators are incentivised to consistently improve their craft and remain current on the most recent educational approaches.*

## Ongoing Educational and Professional Development, as well as Collaboration

*Lesson study* is a practice that is a significant component of the teacher development paradigm that is utilised in Japan. This practice aims to gather instructors together to design, observe, and collaboratively analyse classes to enhance their teaching methods and student outcomes. This type of professional development aims to cultivate a strong sense of community among educators by emphasizing collaboration rather than competition. Teachers work together to evaluate their lessons, discuss how they could be improved, and support one another as they work to implement more effective tactics in the classroom.

"Each class teacher makes it his business to visit the homes of each of his children at least once a year" Ronald P Dore

*Because of its success in promoting innovation in the classroom and enhancing students' learning outcomes, the lesson study technique has garnered acclaim on a global scale. Teachers in Japan foster an atmosphere of continual development by observing one another's pedagogical approaches and providing positive criticism. By working together, educators can improve their teaching strategies to fulfil their pupils' varied requirements better. This strategy also helps cultivate a feeling of shared purpose and accountability.*

*In the same way that Japan is beginning to emphasise teacher training and professional development, India is gradually doing the same. The National Education Policy (NEP) 2020 acknowledges that the quality of instructors directly affects the quality of education that students get. The Indian approach to teacher training, on the other hand, has traditionally placed a greater emphasis on official certifications than on continuous professional development within the teaching profession. India can learn much from Japan's approach to professional collaboration and ongoing professional development for teachers.*

"School remains, for most teachers, not just the place where they earn their bread and butter; it is a place where they belong..." Ronald P Dore

*Adopting a collaborative model of professional development, similar to the lesson study used in Japan, could have a profound impact on the education system in India. Indian schools can cultivate a culture of creativity and quality if they encourage instructors to collaborate, watch each other's teaching methods, and provide feedback to one another. This strategy can alleviate the feelings of loneliness that many educators have as a result of their jobs and establish a network of support for the development of their professional skills.*

*Furthermore, boosting the stature of teachers and reaffirming their role as mentors and guides, rather than merely instructors, could assist in re-establishing the sense of respect and responsibility essential to educational endeavours' success. Teachers are more likely to be driven to improve their abilities and create meaningful learning experiences for their pupils if they have the sense that they are recognised and supported by their colleagues.*

"The reason why Japanese industry works and why Japanese schools teach, why workers don't quit and why children don't drop out of school, is that what is most wanted out of life- stability, security and support- are acquired through effort and commitment." Merry White. This seems to be one good reason why almost nothing can be borrowed from Japan and transplanted to another country where those 3 things are not the most important, and indeed the not quitting thing has started to crack in Japan just as some people have gained other priorities.

*In the Japanese education system, a strong focus is placed on respect for teachers and constant professional growth. This provides India with great lessons to observe. By implementing strategies such as lesson study, in which teachers work together to improve their teaching approaches, Indian educators can improve the overall quality of education and establish a professional community that is more committed to providing support. Furthermore, acknowledging the significant role that instructors play in enhancing students' academic and moral development can help strengthen the relationship between teachers and students, which in turn contributes to the overall development of students.*

"Study, like any activity in Japan worth pursuing, is an opportunity to commit great amounts of effort to a task."
Merry White

# FOUR

## Moral and Character Education

"When engaged effort is valued over ability, the environment of study or work is more truly egalitarian than it would be if the ceiling on a person's efficacy were set by ability alone" The Japanese Educational Challenge by Merry White, pg. 52.

*When I was in Japan, one of the most important things I learned was that the Japanese education system strongly emphasises moral and character education. This is a fundamental component of the Japanese educational system. As opposed to many Western models, which emphasise academic achievement excessively, Japan strikes a balance between academic achievement and the development of well-rounded persons who are conscientious, ethical, and socially responsible. Respect, harmony, and the well-being of the group are two of the cultural values firmly ingrained in this component of their system.*

"The teacher's main concern is that the child be engaged in their work, and not that they be disciplined or docile. Thus, an American teacher might be distressed by the decibel level tolerated." The Japanese Educational Challenge pg. 68. This is something I was very surprised at as I pictured perfectly silent Japanese classrooms, and it turned out to be just the opposite.

## Teaching Morals and Character in Japan's Educational System

*Critical values such as honesty, diligence, respect, and empathy are instilled in Japanese students at a young age and are emphasised throughout their education. These principles are taught in theoretical classes and ingrained in students' daily lives through classroom education, extracurricular activities, and applications relevant to the actual world. The concept that success is not only about individual performance but also about making a constructive contribution to society is reflected in Japan's belief that moral education is recognised as being on par with academic learning in terms of its significance.*

"In mathematics, creative problem solving is emphasized among elementary and lower secondary pupils…" The Japanese Educational Challenge pg. 68. That was another surprise for me and the opposite of my expectations, and is perhaps an explanation for the historical success of Japanese students in maths and science that even Japanese parents might be surprised at.

*As an illustration, students are required to take part in the process of cleaning their classrooms, corridors, and school grounds. This activity is not considered a chore but an integral character development component. By implementing this practice, students are taught the importance of contributing to the group's overall well-being, instilling a sense of responsibility and ownership of their surroundings. Discussions, role-playing activities, and reflections are how moral education is distributed in the classroom. These activities are designed to assist students in internalising these beliefs. Students are encouraged to participate with their communities meaningfully through educational activities and community service initiatives outside of the classroom. These activities serve to highlight the significance of social responsibility.*

"Order, discipline, self-control; it is the school rather than the family which is largely responsible for building these elements into the masculine Japanese character."
Ronald P Dore

*This emphasis on character education cultivates a generation of students who are intellectually capable, empathetic, and aware of their obligations as members of society. Japan's method, which emphasizes harmony rather than competitiveness, teaches students to respect cooperation, empathy, and social advancement rather than individual accomplishment.*

### Instructions for Learning in Indian Schools

*Many important lessons may be learned from Japan's educational system, mainly because India implemented educational reforms through the National Education Policy (NEP) 2020. Although India has achieved tremendous progress in expanding access to education and raising academic standards, there is still space for improvement in terms of Japan's comprehensive approach to development.*

*Here are some essential things to remember:*

*1. The Japanese educational system places a balanced emphasis on academics, extracurricular activities, and moral education. This is one of the most notable aspects of the Japanese educational system. This guarantees that students are academically competent, well-rounded, responsible, and ethical citizens who can contribute to society. India's National*

*Economic Policy 2020 (NEP 2020) emphasizes holistic development, and Japan's approach offers a road map for implementing this vision. It would benefit Indian schools to incorporate more structured character education programs and provide equal attention to cultural activities, sports, and the arts.*

How can we be open-minded?
Ask a question

2. *"Professional Development for Teachers"*: *Japan places significant importance on "continuous professional development" for its*

*teachers and other educators. Teachers continue to engage in activities such as collaborative lesson planning, peer observations, and continual learning to guarantee that they are up to speed with the most recent educational techniques. Not only does this culture of constant improvement increase the overall quality of instruction, but it also allows educators to develop a sense of professionalism. India can embrace this paradigm by increasing the number of opportunities for professional development, mentoring, and continuing education for teachers. Improvements in teacher training and support are necessary to bring about an overall improvement in the quality of education throughout the nation.*

*3. The Japanese educational system is distinguished because it instils a sense of responsibility in pupils at a young age. This is one of the distinctive features of the Japanese educational system. The development of a sense of discipline and respect is fostered in schools through encouraging students to participate in the maintenance of their learning environment. This includes activities such as cleaning classrooms and organising school events. To allow students to take responsibility for their surroundings and their place in the school community, Indian schools should embrace practices analogous to these. Not only would this strengthen their sense of responsibility, but it would also encourage values such as respect for shared areas and the need to work together.*

*4.    "Character    and    Moral    Education":
Incorporating "moral and ethical values" into
the educational curriculum can potentially
boost the formation of responsible citizens
considerably. The National Education Policy
2020 (NEP 2020) of India acknowledges the
significance of character education, and the
model of Japan provides a concrete illustration
of how this can be accomplished. Classroom
discussions, role-playing activities, and real-
world applications such as community service
are some of how schools in India might
concentrate on teaching values such as
empathy, honesty, and respect to their academic
students. It is necessary to consider these ideals
to establish a society that places equal
importance on social harmony and academic
brilliance.*

"...we should hold Japan up as a mirror, not as a blueprint" Good advice on comparing your country to others and trying to borrow ideas, from Merry White

*I gained great insights into the Japanese educational system during my trip to Japan. It combines traditional teaching methods with modern approaches, primarily emphasising pupils' overall growth and development. Japan's commitment to academic rigour and technology integration, focusing on moral and character education, creates an environment where students can achieve in their educational and social endeavours.*

*Japan's model provides India with several guiding principles as it pursues the reforms described in the National Economic Policy 2020. If the country adopts a more holistic approach to education, emphasises continuous teacher development, and encourages student responsibility, it can produce a new generation of students who are academically accomplished, ethical, compassionate, and prepared to contribute positively to society.*

# FIVE

# Technology and Innovation in Japanese Classrooms

*India may learn from Japan's education system because it offers a unique blend of deeply established traditions and cutting-edge technical breakthroughs. This is a balance that India can learn from, especially as it embraces the aims of the National Education Policy (NEP) 2020. Even though Japan is well-known for its reverence for traditional teaching techniques, the country is also noted for its forward-thinking approach to incorporating cutting-*

edge technology into educational settings. During my trip to Japanese schools, I had the opportunity to watch this delicate balance in action. This equilibrium can serve as a model for how India should navigate the process of incorporating technology into its educational system.

## Utilisation of Technology for a Specific Purpose

*The classrooms I saw in Japan had interactive whiteboards, iPads, and various other digital tools designed to make the learning process easier. On the other hand, what stood out was that technology was not the focal point; instead, it was a tool used to enhance learning rather than replace more conventional ways. The educators in Japan are aware that although technology has the potential to make education more accessible and exciting, it must be utilised with a purpose and in moderation to achieve the desired results. The primary focus continues to be ensuring pupils get a solid foundation in fundamental academic topics such as mathematics, science, and literacy.*

*This method ensures that students do not become unduly dependent on digital resources but instead use them to enhance their comprehension of fundamental theoretical concepts. Tablets, for instance, were utilised in mathematics classes to allow students to engage in interactive problem-solving activities. However, teachers continued to emphasize more conventional approaches to problem-solving. By integrating technology, students can improve their critical thinking skills while increasing their engagement and motivation.*

### *Education in the STEM fields and technological competence*

*Education focusing on STEM (science,*

*technology, engineering, and mathematics) is becoming increasingly popular in Japan. The Japanese government recognises that the future economy will require workers who are knowledgeable in these fields and able to apply their knowledge to problems in the contemporary world.*

*In several of the schools I visited, children were participating in activities related to advanced technology projects, robotics, and coding. These activities encouraged students to investigate ideas such as engineering, artificial intelligence, and automation at a young age.*

*Through the curriculum's emphasis on STEM (science, technology, engineering, and mathematics), students in Japan are encouraged to develop problem-solving, critical thinking, and creative skills, which helps them prepare for occupations in which technical competency will be essential. Incorporating these fields into Japan's educational system demonstrates a forward-thinking approach, as it acknowledges that these competencies will be necessary for the country's continued economic success.*

*The implementation of this strategy offers Indian educators and policymakers a roadmap for cultivating a generation of technology-proficient individuals while simultaneously ensuring that creativity and critical thinking continue to play a vital role in the educational process.*

## *The process of bridging the digital divide in India*

*India can absorb great lessons from Japan's careful technology integration, which, combined with its respect for traditional learning techniques, presents India with valuable teachings. Even though the National Education Policy 2020 (NEP 2020) is bringing about significant changes to India's educational system, the digital gap remains a significant obstacle. Compared to urban schools, which may have more advanced digital tools but lack purposeful integration, many rural communities still do not have access to even the most fundamental technical infrastructure components. Japan's paradigm demonstrates how technology may improve learning without stifling fundamental educational goals.*

*In India, it is of the utmost importance to use technology to bridge this difference. This involves ensuring that all students have access to digital tools while simultaneously ensuring that these technologies supplement traditional learning techniques rather than replace them. The Japanese model emphasises the significance of consciously utilising technology, enhancing the students' existing knowledge, fostering teamwork, and preparing them for future problems.*

*While India is moving forward with education reforms under NEP 2020, the education system in Japan is a valuable case study for India to consider. The deliberate application of technology in Japan's classrooms, combined with the increased emphasis on STEM education, offers a balanced approach for teaching professionals in India to learn. This is true, although both countries have unique cultural traditions. Japan's model of employing digital tools to enhance rather than replace conventional learning while also cultivating vital skills for the future should serve as a source of inspiration for India as it works to incorporate technology into its educational system. Implementing this strategy will assist India in preparing its students for the future while tackling the issues brought by the digital divide.*

# SIX

## LESSONS FOR INDIAN EDUCATION

One of the most well-known aspects of the Japanese education system is its well-structured and well-balanced approach to academic accomplishment, character development, and overall developmental growth. India can learn significant lessons from Japan's practices, mainly as it implements the National Education Policy (NEP) 2020. These teachings are deeply embedded in Japan's distinctive cultural background, but India can learn from Japan's practices. Adjusting these procedures carefully could result in a considerable improvement to the Indian educational system.

***First and foremost, self-control and accountability***

*The fact that Japanese schools strongly focus on self-discipline and responsibility is one of the most remarkable elements of Japanese education. Not only are students accountable for their academic work, but they are also accountable for maintaining the cleanliness and upkeep of their classrooms and the overall school environment. A sense of ownership and pride in their surroundings is instilled via self-management, which also encourages the development of teamwork. The act of cleaning is not regarded as a chore but rather as an essential component of the daily routine at the school, which teaches students to respect shared spaces and be committed to the community's well-being.*

*Indian schools can use analogous procedures to instil a sense of responsibility and discipline in children. To assist kids in acquiring vital life skills such as teamwork, leadership, and a strong work ethic, it is beneficial to encourage them to participate in maintaining their environment. This can be accomplished through activities such as cleaning or organising school events. Implementing such routines can cultivate a stronger connection between students and the setting in which they are learning, thus fostering respect and accountability.*

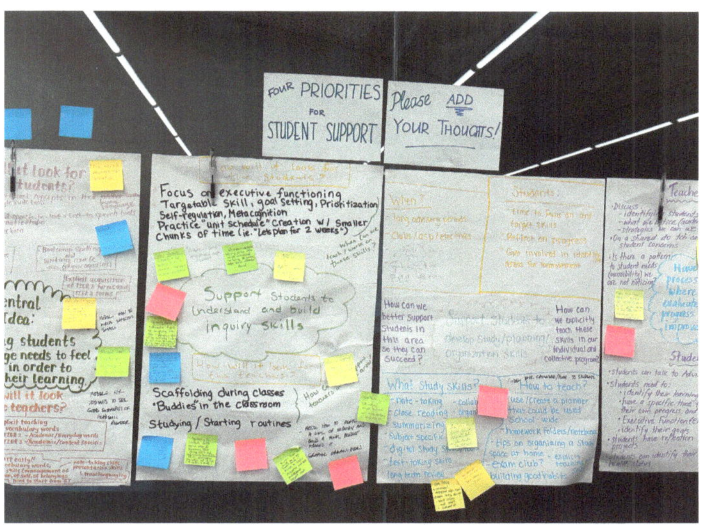

## *Education in Moral Precepts*

*It is a fundamental component of Japan's educational system to provide pupils with moral education, intending to transform them into well-rounded and ethical individuals. The significance of moral principles, respect for others, and social duty is instilled in Japanese children at a young age and continues throughout their education. This character education is incorporated into the curriculum seamlessly to ensure that students develop into responsible citizens who make a constructive contribution to society.*

*Education on moral and ethical principles has always been a primary priority in India, yet there is an opportunity for more profound incorporation into the learning process in everyday life. Schools can emulate Japan's approach by including classes focusing on character development in the curriculum. For instance, lessons on topics such as empathy, respect for diversity, and social responsibility can be incorporated into social studies, language, and even science courses. Given that NEP 2020 places an emphasis on holistic development, implementing moral education methods has the potential to assist in cultivating a new generation of ethical and socially conscious citizens.*

## Professional Development Opportunities for Teachers

*The Japanese educational system considers teacher professional development an essential component. Teachers typically participate in collaborative lesson preparation, peer reviews, and other activities. This ongoing process of learning and growth contributes to maintaining high teaching standards and encouraging innovative teaching practices within the class setting.*

*The use of such approaches can be of*

*considerable help to Indian schools. Sharing ideas, refining teaching strategies, and improving the overall quality of education are all things that may be accomplished when teachers are encouraged to engage in collaborative lesson preparation and mutual evaluation. The National Education Policy 2020 (NEP 2020) emphasises the importance of continual professional development. Adopting a model comparable to Japan's makes it possible to ensure that Indian educators are adequately equipped to fulfil the ever-changing requirements of students in the 21ˢᵗ century.*

### Focus on Holistic Development as the Fourth Priority

*The school system in Japan lays a significant focus on holistic development, making it a priority to ensure that pupils not only achieve academically but also flourish in extracurricular activities. The stress linked with academic pressures is reduced when schools encourage kids to participate in sports, arts, and cultural activities. This helps to build well-rounded development and minimises the resulting stress. Students are allowed to explore their interests, grow their confidence, and develop essential life skills such as leadership and teamwork by implementing this balanced approach.*

*Implementing a similar strategy in Indian*

*schools would be beneficial since it would ensure students have adequate opportunities to participate in extracurricular activities and academic pursuits. Schools can incorporate extracurricular activities into their curriculums more comprehensively, as the National Education Policy 2020 acknowledges the significance of holistic development. The Indian education system has the potential to assist students in developing into well-rounded individuals who are confidently equipped to meet problems in both the academic realm and the real world. This is accomplished by promoting sports, arts, and cultural interests.*

*The country's cultural setting moulds the educational system in Japan; nonetheless, many of the approaches used in Japan can provide India with valuable insights for its efforts to reform its educational system. It is possible to establish a learning environment that is more balanced and productive by emphasizing things like moral education, ethical education, teacher development, and holistic growth. These lessons from Japan can inspire improvements that cultivate individuals who are well-rounded, responsible, and capable and who are prepared for the needs of a world that is fast changing. India is currently in the process of implementing the National Education Policy 2020.*

# SEVEN

## CONCLUSION

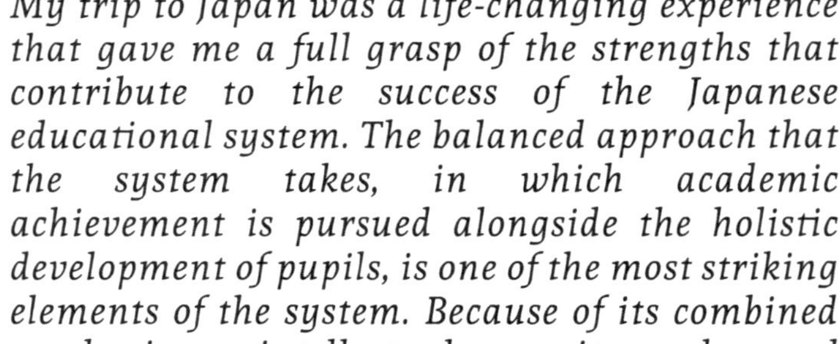

*My trip to Japan was a life-changing experience that gave me a full grasp of the strengths that contribute to the success of the Japanese educational system. The balanced approach that the system takes, in which academic achievement is pursued alongside the holistic development of pupils, is one of the most striking elements of the system. Because of its combined emphasis on intellectual capacity and moral character, Japan's educational approach is not only practical but also profoundly significant in preparing students for the problems they will face in their lives, both professionally and personally.*

*Exceptional academic performance with the cultivation of moral character*

*Japan's educational system strongly emphasises academic rigour while concurrently encouraging the development of essential traits such as self-control, responsibility, and moral rectitude. Students' respect for their professors and the learning environment fosters an environment in which they are inspired to achieve success not only for themselves but also as a component of the more extraordinary social fabric. In Japan, teachers are considered mentors because they are responsible for imparting information and life skills to their students. One practice that stands out as one that should be emulated is the commitment that schools have made to promoting ethical behaviour and personal responsibility.*

*As we negotiate the changes brought about by the National Education Policy (NEP) 2020 in India, this combination of academic accomplishment and character formation can serve as a guiding principle. Although Indian education has traditionally emphasized the acquisition of knowledge, incorporating moral education into the curriculum can assist in developing well-rounded individuals. This integration can occur in subtle, everyday behaviours, such as encouraging students to clean their classrooms and developing teamwork through group activities and projects, as demonstrated by the Japanese model, emphasising how this integration can occur.*

*Integration of Technology and Innovation in that Technology*

*One more important thing that may be learnt from Japan is how well it incorporates technology into the educational system. It is awe-inspiring that the nation is emphasising using technology as a tool to enhance learning rather than replacing traditional instruction methods. Every classroom is outfitted with cutting-edge digital tools, and students are actively encouraged to interact with technology in ways that contribute to improving their educational experience. Instruction in coding, as well as the utilisation of virtual reality in teaching history or science, are examples of how technology is considered a facilitator of more profound learning.*

*In India, where the National Education Policy 2020 (NEP 2020) places a large focus on technology and digital literacy, Japan's model provides useful insights. Indian schools can overcome geographical and infrastructural constraints by thoughtfully and deliberately utilising technology in classrooms. This will also help pupils prepare for a digital future. To guarantee that technology does not replace the personal touch that instructors bring to the classroom, it is essential to ensure that it complements it.*

*A reverence for the principles of responsibility and discipline*

*The Japanese educational system strongly emphasizes responsibility and discipline, which is one of its most motivating components. Students are expected to take responsibility for their learning environment, providing assistance to their classmates, keeping their supplies organized, and maintaining a clean atmosphere. This instils a sense of accountability at a young age, which gradually becomes a valuable talent.*

*Incorporating such tasks into everyday routines can produce more self-reliant, disciplined, and socially conscious pupils. This is especially true in India, where academic results are frequently spotlighted. Because of its focus on holistic education, the National Education Policy 2020 presents an ideal chance to implement comparable approaches.*

*Insights from Japan can serve as significant precedents for reform, and India is also embarking on the revolutionary journey of the New Economic Policy 2020 (NEP 2020). Japan provides lessons that have the potential to improve the quality of education in India significantly. These lessons include the promotion of discipline and responsibility, the integration of academic achievement and character development, and the effective utilisation of technology. Creating an education system that not only prepares kids for academic achievement but also moulds them into responsible and capable citizens of the future is something that we may strive to achieve by carefully adapting these approaches.*

www.authordheerajmehrotra.com

# EIGHT

## JIT In Education

*Within the realm of academia, the Just-In-Time (JIT) concept of Japan has been incorporated.*

*The Just-In-Time (JIT) concept is a methodology that emphasises efficiency by manufacturing only what is needed, when it is needed, and in the exact amount that is required. This concept was pioneered by Japanese firms such as Toyota. While this idea has typically been utilised in the manufacturing industry to cut down on waste and boost efficiency, it can also be efficiently implemented in academic settings to improve the current teaching, learning, and administrative procedures.*

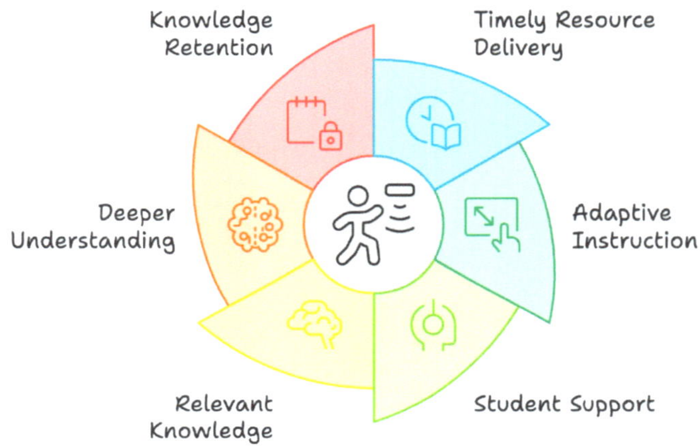



www.authordheerajmehrotra.com

## An Explanation of Just-In-Time (JIT) in the Context of Academics

*In the field of education, the JIT approach refers to the practice of providing students with learning resources, instruction, and support at precisely the moment when they require them. A style of education that is both flexible and effective is advocated for here. This approach ensures that students are not inundated with material but rather acquire pertinent knowledge at the appropriate time, promoting deeper comprehension and retention.*

In the traditional style of education, students are typically required to study a substantial quantity of material all at once, regardless of when they will put that information to use. JIT is a strategy that addresses this issue by guaranteeing that students acquire knowledge that is instantly applicable, so producing a learning process that is more dynamic and entertaining.

JIT's Advantages in the Academic World

One of the most essential advantages of just-in-time (JIT) in the field of education is the decrease of academic clutter, which leads to increased efficiency. Teachers can condense lesson plans and concentrate on the most essential subject, deleting anything that is either unneeded or out of date. This results in more focused learning, in which students receive only the required knowledge at the appropriate time, increasing the likelihood that they will retain and use the information.

2. Personalised Learning: Just-in-time (JIT) allows for more individualised learning experiences to be created. Educators can make content and support available to students based on their specific requirements when they assess the development of pupils in real-time. For instance, instead of bombarding students with several concepts, teachers can introduce new

*information as soon as students demonstrate that they are ready for the next step. The fact that each student can go at their own pace is another way this strategy helps differentiate instruction in the classroom.*

*3. The importance of learning is emphasised by JIT, which has a positive impact on education. Students engage with content that they can immediately put to use, as opposed to acquiring abstract concepts that have no immediate application. The learning experience can be made more relevant by, for instance, introducing students to mathematical formulas while they are working on specific problem-solving activities. This is an alternative to the traditional method of memorising mathematical formulas without comprehending how they are applied.*

*The Just-In-Time (JIT) methodology, which has its origins in the industrial sector, can also be utilised for resource management in educational institutions. Educational institutions can implement JIT to manage educational resources, such as textbooks, technology, and teaching aids, to guarantee that these resources are accessible when they are required, without the need to overstock or waste items. This aligns with sustainability goals and lessens administrative matters' costs.*

*When it comes to academics, implementing JIT*

*1. Curriculum Design: To support JIT principles, the curriculum needs to be adaptable and modular throughout its entirety. With a modular curriculum, teachers can present pupils with more manageable and smaller bits of information at the precise moment when they are ready to acquire them. This approach has the potential to be especially useful in fields such as physics and mathematics, where more complicated ideas are constructed on top of an existing foundation of knowledge.*

*2. Integration of Technology: The implementation of just-in-time (JIT) in academic settings is significantly aided by the use of digital platforms and learning management systems (LMS). Technology makes it possible to evaluate students' learning progress in real time, which assists teachers in determining whether a student is ready to learn new content. For example, AI-powered learning platforms can provide materials or task recommendations based on each student's performance.*

*Teacher Training: For Just-in-Time (JIT) to be successful, teachers must receive training in adaptive teaching practices. It is expected that they would be able to swiftly evaluate the requirements of their students and modify their teaching methods accordingly. JIT's effectiveness in the classroom is contingent upon the implementation of professional development programs that have an emphasis on real-time evaluation, decision-making that is driven by data, and variable instructional strategies.*

*4. Collaboration and Communication: Teachers, students, and parents need to have good communication to implement JIT in the educational setting. Students are guaranteed to receive the appropriate amount of support at the proper moment when they receive continuous feedback. Teachers can work with their colleagues to facilitate the exchange of best practices and modify educational tactics based on their students' performance.*

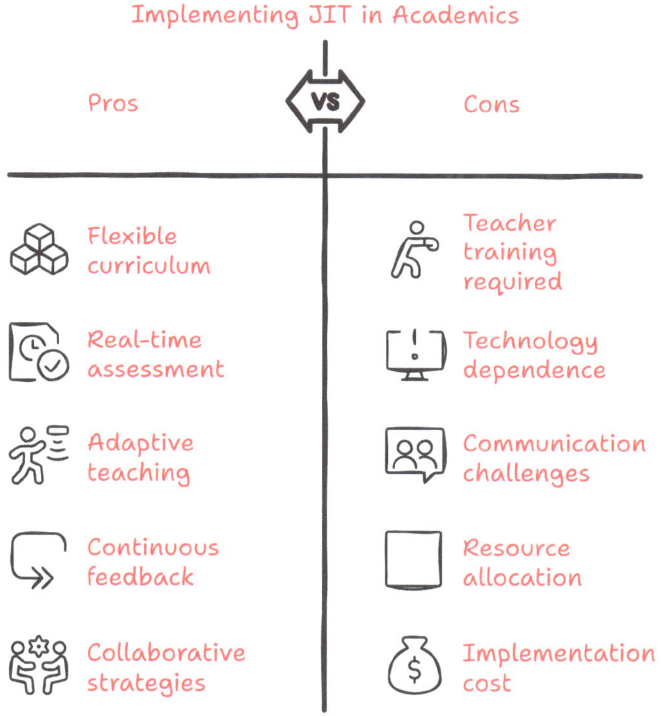


## *Obstacles and Things to Take Into Account*

*The implementation of JIT in academic settings does provide specific difficulties. It is necessary to make a cultural shift in how education is usually seen, moving away from rigid, time-bound systems and towards models that are more fluid and adaptable of their nature. There is a possibility that schools will be resistant to change, and teachers might require some time to adjust to the flexibility that JIT requires. In addition, the necessary infrastructure, which includes technology and data management systems, must be in place to support this strategy.*

*The implementation of the Just-In-Time (JIT) methodology in the realm of education gives a chance to develop learning environments that are more effective, individualised, and pertinent. Schools can improve student engagement, minimise inefficiencies, and encourage a deeper grasp of subject matter when they give content and resources when required. Providing students with the resources they require at the precise moment they need them is the goal of the Just-In-Time (JIT) approach, which has the potential to become a cornerstone of future-focused academic models as education continues to transform.*

# About The Author

*Dheeraj Mehrotra, MS, MPhil, PhD (Education Management)., a white and a yellow belt in SIX SIGMA, a Certified NLP Business Diploma holder, is an Educational Innovator, Author, with expertise in Six Sigma In Education, Academic Audits, Neuro-Linguistic Programming (NLP), Total Quality Management In Education, an Experiential Educator, a CBSE Resource towards School Assessment (SQAA), CCE, JIT, Five S, and KAIZEN. He has authored over 100 books on computer science, AI, digital body language, NLP, quality circles, school management, classroom effectiveness, and safety and security. A former Principal at De Indian Public School, New Delhi, (INDIA), NPS International School, Guwahati, and Education Officer at GEMS, Gurgaon, with ample teaching experience of over Three Decades, he is a certified Trainer for Quality Circles/ TQM in Education and QCI Standards for School Accreditation/ School Audits and Management. He has also been honoured with the President of India's National Teacher Award in 2006 and the Best Science Teacher State Award (By the Ministry of Science and Technology, State of UP), Innovation in Education for his inception of Six Sigma In Education by Education Watch, New Delhi and Education World- Best Teacher*

Award, BOLT Learner Teacher Award by Air India, 'Innovation in Education Award 2016' by Higher Education Forum (HEF), Gujarat Chapter, among others. He has developed over 150 FREE EDUCATIONAL MOBILE Apps for the Google Play Store exclusively for Teachers, Students, and Parents. This work has been recognised by the LIMCA BOOK OF RECORDS and INDIA BOOK OF RECORDS as the only Indian to draw that feast. As a founder president of the IoT Society of India, he also promotes Technology Globally. Dr Mehrotra is presently engaged as a PRINCIPAL at KUNWARS GLOBAL SCHOOL, Lucknow, India. He has conducted over 2000 workshops globally on "Excellence In Education" integrated with Total Quality Management and Six Sigma, Technology Integration in Education (TIE), Developing towards being ROCKSTAR TEACHERS, including Cyberspace, Cyber Security, Classroom Management, School Leadership & Management, and Innovative teaching within classrooms via Mind Maps, NLP and Experiential Learning in Academics. He is an active TEDx speaker and can be viewed on the YouTube TEDx channel. As a premium UDEMY Instructor, he has developed over 500 courses and caters to over 8 Lakh students from 180 countries. He can be visited at www.authordheerajmehrotra.com

# Books By The Same Author

@Amazon